All Scripture references taken from the KJV of the Holy Bible, unless otherwise indicated.

Choose an Altar, *To Choose a Church*

by Dr. Marlene Miles

Freshwater Press 2024

freshwaterpress9@gmail.com

ISBN: 978-1-965772-00-3

Paperback Version

Copyright 2024, Dr. Marlene Miles

All rights reserved. No part of this book may be reproduced, distributed, or transmitted by any means or in any means including photocopying, recording or other electronic or mechanical methods without prior written permission of the publisher except in the case of brief publications or critical reviews.

Table of Contents

On The Altar 5
The People in the Church 12
You Choose Altars All the Time 16
You Don't Go to Evil Altars 30
The Public Altar 34
Common Altars 39
God Loves a Good Altar 42
Kings & Altars 46
God Hates an Evil Altar 49
Kings & Priests 54
Priesting At an Altar 57
Family Altar, Family Priest 61
Forgetfulness 65
Fake Churches 77
Deceived Churches 80
A Good Altar Is Hard to Find 89
A Priest Forever 94
Deceived People 101
Judge an Altar 104
Occultic, Undercover Altar 108
Choose By the Altar 115

On This Revelation 119
Dear Reader 122
Prayer books by this author 123
Other books by this author 127
Other Series 137

Choose An Altar
to choose a church

On The Altar

The fire on the altar shall be kept burning on it; it shall not go out. The priest shall burn wood on it every morning, and he shall arrange the burnt offering on it and shall burn on it the fat of the peace offerings.
(Leviticus 6:12 ESV)

One day near the end of February of this year, I was reading in the Old Testament how the Israelites offered sacrifices to Jehovah. They had sacrifices going 24/7, every day, certain times of day and double or more on certain holidays and feast days. Like you, I'd read that before, perhaps multiple times before, but this particular day I really saw what was on the page; and it registered in my spirit.

Immediately I thought that maybe I was missing out on something, by not sacrificing every day, but instead, just on Sundays, on some Bible Study nights, and every now and again when I watched an online video that stirred me, where I felt either excited or obligated to bless the speaker.

So, the Lord put it on my heart to put something on the altar every day in the month of March. This was February 25th, but as soon as I got the green light to begin doing this for the month of March, I ended up starting right away at the end of February.

I won't tell you play-by-play or day-by-day what happened, but I can summarize what I discovered by offering a sacrifice every day of the month for one month.

One of the main reasons that I made daily sacrifice was to judge the altar of the place of worship that I was attending. Were the Israelites getting a result and a benefit that I had never experienced? I really wanted to know, and I really wanted to experience God in a deeper way and I felt that sacrificing was a way to get there.

As I set out on this endeavor, as much as it was in me and by help of the Holy Spirit I walked uprightly before the Lord. I tried my utmost to be diligent in shunning sin, reading and studying the Bible, praying, praising, and worshipping. I tried to be conscientious at work and treating family, coworkers, and people, in general, right.

That was the laver. Along with repentance I kept my hands as clean as possible and watched that my feet did not go any unclean place. My placing sacrifice on the altar daily was to judge the altar, not to judge my faithfulness, generosity, or obedience, so I had to behave myself well.

Churches are places of fellowship. They are places of worship. They are Houses of Prayer. And, my friends, they are designated as the Tabernacle of the

Lord where there is a laver basin and an altar. Although spiritual now, those things are in the tent of meetings or the tabernacle of the Lord so we must behave ourselves well.

I was, with at least permission and possibly by the direction of the Lord, testing the altar of the church I attended. What was revealed to me was not only astounding, but it has also propelled me to write this book and to admonish all who go to "church"--, any kind of church to choose their church by its **altar** more than by any of the other many parameters.

When looking for a church there are many choices. Some cities have a church or what looks like a church on every corner. There are some that are historic, some are elegant. Some are basic and primitive. Some are classical. Others are so contemporary inside they look like movie theatres or concert halls. The choices seem endless. In some warmer cultures that have large followings they actually do use tents. While we should desire to have a beautiful setting for the Lord's House, where the Spirit of the Lord is, is *church* in my opinion. If the Holy Spirit is present, it is church, no matter what the edifice looks like.

Then the next level of decision, what are the people like inside? Do they dress up there, or are they casual? Are they regular people or are they really rich?

Then the next level, what is the praise and worship like? What is the music like?

And the preacher, what is he or she like? Is there preaching, teaching, or just Ted Talks?

Sadly, most of us stop there. Do we like the church. Do we like the location? Is it nice inside? Are the people nice or at least do they not irritate us? Is the music *krunk*? Does the preacher's preaching not offend? Then we may feel that this is a **safe** place to be and *join*. But is it really safe?

What have you *joined* if you only looked at external markers?

How will this "church" help your Christianity? How will it minister to your spirit man? How will it restore your soul? How will it affect your family? How will it affect your health and prosperity?

If you haven't given any of that a thought, then you are not planning for this "church" to do any of that for you. Are you planning on Jesus to magically do everything no matter what church you go to? Or, are you planning to do it yourself, a DIY Christian walk? Some things in your Christian walk you must do for yourself, but not everything. God says we should be fitly joined together. This is why He put gifts in the Church so we could help one another.

Are you planning to do what you've always done, and the church is just something you do on Sunday, so you don't look like a heathen to your neighbors, or get in trouble with Grandma who told you that you **had** to go to church? Or, is it for your social life, or maybe for your conscience?

Then you are planning for your church to be an accessory to your life, not an integral part of it. If that is the case, then you are likely to think that it doesn't matter what church you go to. Let me say that even if you don't intend to really participate in the church you attend then you may logically think it doesn't matter. If you don't think the church will impact your life, you are seriously mistaken. Keep reading to find out how much the church you choose and attend, whether you participate fully or not affects you, your life, your future, your destiny, and your children and *their* children.

The People in the Church

Yes, we look at the people. We must look at the people who 1 into that church as well as the people who come out. We must look at their condition when they come in and their condition when they leave. This speaks of what *conversion* and what transformation happens or can happen in that church. There is a corporate anointing that affects the entire congregation; the anointing makes the difference.

The **church** doesn't change a person; Jesus does and the person's letting Jesus have access to them to change them is how conversion really comes about.

Is Jesus in that church? Is Jesus allowed in that church? Is He invited? Is Jesus preached in that church? Then, Hallelujah.

There is a Godly anointing with the Holy Spirit, however, there is a demonic anointing with other *spirits*. The **anointing** in that church is what will change the people who go there. The Spirit of the Lord is invoked and influences the altar of that place. If He is not and other *spirits* are running amok in there, those spirits will affect the people of that place.

So, what's in that church? What Spirit is in the church you attend? The Holy Spirit? Or, not? This is how you identify the altar and what altar is working in the House of Prayer that you are a member of.

Looking at these factors is a good start to see what happens in that church. Not the daily, weekly, or monthly events, planned and executed by the humans there, but what happens *spiritually* in that church based on the fact that it is a church, is proclaimed to be a church, and has an altar—well, at least one altar. And, by virtue of that altar the Spirit of God is invoked and comes into the services there.

We should look to see what happens to the people and the families who go there because of going to that church and connecting to the **altar** of that church, if any.

And immediately his fame spread abroad throughout all the region round about Galilee. (Mark 1:28)

When a parent is looking for the college for their teen to enroll in, they look for the reputation of that school. What does the child want to be? What does the student want to accomplish scholastically and career-wise? Then the best school where that can be realized is chosen. When the *fame* of a college is they put out good teachers, or good lawyers is known, those who want to pursue that profession or career will apply to that university.

When the fame of Jesus began to spread abroad, even though He did not come to Earth to make a reputation for Himself, people came in multitudes to hear Him speak and also to be healed.

When the "fame" of a college or university becomes evident, by the kinds of professionals they matriculate, then people who want what that college offers will apply and attend there. When the *fame* of a **church** becomes known, it should by that fame and by the Spirit begin to attract those who want what that church is offering.

One of the main people to look at is the pastor. Pray hard about this because he is the main priest of that house. Look at the people he most intimately priests to--, his wife, his children--, his family.

We will give the pastor and his family a whole chapter later in this book, but for now we can keep talking about other things.

You Choose Altars All the Time

You choose altars all the time, every day. Sometimes you know you're going to an altar, sometimes you may not realize it.
How so?
Altars are everywhere.
We go to people's houses, to various locations and businesses all the time, but we may not realize that these places are **altars** or *have* altars. Churches are not the only places with altars. An altar could be inside or outside of a building. Not realizing that they are altars we may not know if they are Godly or evil altars.

We most often can tell how we *feel* about a place when we get there and start to look around. Is it "normal" in there? Is it dark and creepy? Is it light and lively? These are the first clues. Next, we may evaluate how we **feel**. Do we feel good? Do we feel scared? Do we feel withdrawn, as though we don't belong there, and want to leave?

What we may be experiencing is the spiritual makeup of a place in our own spirit, via the Holy Spirit. The spiritual makeup of a place is determined by what *spirits* are there--, which ones are allowed or invited there, and which ones are banned or not allowed in that place. The infusing of spirits, or the "vibe" of a place happens because of an altar, or altars that may be present.

We may not visibly see anything that looks like an altar, but your discerning spirit man can detect the spiritual makeup of a place if you are sharpened in your discernment, and paying attention. So, this place that you've entered is an altar, or has at least one altar, and the Holy Spirit in you is talking. It is best to ask, but many times the Holy Spirit will tell you need-to-know information without you even asking.

Be quiet for a moment and **listen**.
Feel.
***Pray*.**
Listen. What does He say?

If the Holy Spirit says get out of there, then leave. Leave right away. I have left places that *looked* normal but by unction of the Spirit of God I was to leave, so I left. There could have been absolutely nothing wrong with that place, from all *appearances*. But there could have been everything wrong with that place **for me**, that day, that hour, that moment. I was not alerted to tell anyone else to leave so there wasn't imminent danger to the building or the denizens there; I was just unctioned to leave.

In this way we recognize that we can't do what everyone else is doing all the time. We must do what God is urging us, many times, individually, by His Spirit to do. This is for our safety and protection.

You wouldn't purposefully go to an evil altar, would you?

How can you know that you went to an evil altar if you weren't even planning to go to one?

First of all, you should know what altars are evil... fortune tellers, astrologers, witch doctors, spiritual and energy healers, New Age, witch's covens, tarot or any other card reading, are grown up examples of places with evil altars. Ouija Board as a kid or an adult is an altar that is designed to invoke a *familiar spirit* and interface the spiritual with the physical realms, but by demonic means.

False teachers, preachers, and prophets have evil altars, are evil altars themselves, or priest over evil altars if they are the head of or in positions of leadership in a "church."

The clues could be right in front of you. The place is spooky, creepy, has demonic or satanic symbols and artifacts on a table, for example, a pentagram painted on the wall or the floor, and or strewn about the place. Looks witchy. Looks occultic. The person may or may not have planned for the place to look that way, they may just be drawn to acquire and collect those items, over time, by the *spirits* that live in their soul. It could be so subtle that the person may not even realize that they are transforming their place to look witchy or satanic. For example, **demons love red and black**. Some occultic priests have marks and tattoos on themselves, wear witchy attire and jewelry. Look closely, but be discreet.

Look around your own home and in your own closet and jewelry box. You may begin to see with new eyes that some of the things you have are not Godly things and may be attracting demonic things to you. Pray and ask the Holy Spirit to show you those things that attract evil *spirits*, and how to pray over those things, to consecrate them. Some things cannot be consecrated for Godly use and should be discarded. Pray to find out what things you own should be removed, and **how** to remove and get rid of them.

Often, places like this are hidden or tucked away. Or the person who greets you there has a witchy or warlocky vibe. If you don't have the Holy Spirit, you may not pick up on any of that. Especially if there is also a Holy Bible displayed somewhere in that set up.

A Holy Bible?

Oh yeah, that Bible is not only placed there to deceive the people who come in there, it is used by the person when they get scared out of their own wits for going too far into the dark world of demons and then realize they are in too deep, and the demons are out of control. Yes, they have the nerve to call on God. In this way, many believe they are clever, wiser than most, and straddling both the kingdom of darkness and the Kingdom of Light.

They are not. A demon may *let* you think you are lording over them, but without Christ what do you think you will get a demon to do?

God is Merciful but He will not always strive with man. God is most likely dealing according to, *Forgive them they don't know what they do*. Once those who practice the occult are hardened, and they really know what they are doing, they may look for God, but they won't find Him. God is not playing, folks.

Those who "priest" over an evil altar, invoke demons, devils, and idol *gods*. These disembodied spirits, once brought up from hell are looking for homes. Humans are "homes" to them. *Did you know that **homie**?* These *spirits* follow people home from evil altars seeking a chance to get into their souls.

Another way you can know that you went to an evil altar is by the way the person behind the charms, crystal ball, or what have you speaks. They may say the word, *god*, but what "god" are they talking about? **You cannot call GOD using a**

defiled, evil, demonic, satanic, occultic, or witchy altar.

Will they say Jesus Christ, or allude to Jesus in His lordship, messiahship at all? Will they say the Blood of Jesus? You may not be listening for those words, because you may already know you didn't come expecting to hear those words. If you came expecting a quick fix, or to put a quick hit on someone, then don't pretend that you don't know where you are when you are at an evil altar.

You may not have known that you went to an evil altar; it may not look evil, dark, spooky or anything like that. It could look normal or even pretty. It could look like a regular house. It could look like a regular "church," but the altar behind the curtain is not of God, and neither is the priest, nor the *wizard* behind the curtain of God?

Now pray. What is the *spirit* of that place? You need spiritual vision, a discerning spirit, a prayerful mode and ears to hear what the Holy Spirit tells you. What happens to or has happened to the people who are in that place or have been in that place? What does their Fruit look like? Who have they become? Are their children a hot mess, or are they richly blessed?

When I refer to an altar as being witchy, or dark, hidden, or occultic as an evil altar, I must say that you could be at a church that seems like a great place but if there is NO POWER from the altar, that altar is weak. If that altar cannot protect you or fight for you, and win spiritual battles for you, why are you still attending that place? No, I'm not talking about signs, wonders, miracles, and theater. I'm not talking about entertainment; I'm talking about the power of God flowing into your life to be sure you defeat every enemy that comes up against you.

Let God arise and let His enemies be scattered, in the Name of Jesus (Psalm 68:1). Is that happening for you? Is God arising when you pray? Are your enemies being scattered? Then, good; you're at the right altar.

You may never have known that you went to an evil altar, but maybe you did. You may never have known that you went to several in a day, or every day, but they are out there. Do you have any idea how many shops, restaurants, and nail salons, especially those in other countries have charms and good luck stuff over their doors or in other places in their establishments to promote sales and business success? In your vacation travel you may see something "different" in a place and think how charming. Yeah, it's charming alright; it might **be** an outright *charm*. You may think it's so unique that you want to take a picture of it, or with it. You may want to buy it and take it home, so you do. Did you pray about it, first? It's like drinking the water in a foreign place—it may be fine for those who live there, were born there, and grew up there, but it may tear your insides up. Pray, first, then travel. Pray, then partake of "different" things such as vacation souvenirs and even the food while at home and abroad.

Those places have evil altars; when you patronize them you are participating in worshipping the entities that they are worshipping. Imagine what you are bringing home when you visit strange places with strange altars, and especially if you bring their "stuff" into your house as décor or food, or clothing and accessories for your body. Ever thought about that?

Be sure to sanctify and dedicate everything you bring into your home for yourself and your family. Bless it before use.

Maybe you didn't even leave home, but an evil altar came to you. There are mobile altars; animals can be altars; *people* can be altars. Some people's celebrity status is so intense, and even their purpose in life and their livelihood is dependent on them being worshipped; they are altars.

Really?
They seek to be idolized.
Really? Such as?
Such as most celebrities you see on TV and in the movies. If they are not idolized and adored who will buy their records, or go to their concerts? What is a concert stage? Is it an altar? You tell me.

An altar is where the physical interfaces with the spiritual. It is a place of worship. Like Jacob's ladder, the "angels" go up and down. It is a place of sacrifice. Are you there to receive a blessing, offer a sacrifice, or unwittingly **_be_** a sacrifice? How many people "randomly" die at huge festivals and concerts? One is too many; people shouldn't die at a concert.

Be careful, saints of God; there are some places, some altars you should **never** go to, for any reason.

You tell me what happens at a rock or other concert. If you are idolizing the band and or the singer, is the stage not an altar? If the singer is "channeling" their "muse" or whatever *god* they get their sounds, songs, and beats from, is that not the physical interfacing with the spirit realm? There's nothing new under the sun, so where did they get this *new* stuff from?

Did you spend money and now time and attention on this show? Money is a sacrifice. Is this not an altar? Is this altar to God? If not then it is an evil altar.

Make sure **you** are not an altar, demanding worship from a person or people.

A newlywed man in bridegroom enthusiasm told his new wife that he worships her. She scolded him, not wanting to get into any trouble with God, she said, *"See that you do it not."* He became perturbed with her and that was the end of the marriage. (I don't make this stuff up.)

> And I, John saw these things, and heard them. And when I had heard and seen, I fell down to worship before the feet of the angel which shewed me these things.

Then saith he unto me, See thou do it not: for I am thy fellowservant, and of thy brethren the prophets, and of them which keep the sayings of this book: worship God. (Revelations 22:8-9)

We don't worship people. We don't worship angels. We don't worship things; we worship God. Mind the words of the Angel: **Worship God.**

Careful of people who worship you, or feign worship, they are usually after something from you. Beware of flattery, the Word says.

...a flattering mouth worketh ruin
(Proverbs 26:28b)

You Don't Go to Evil Altars

You don't go to evil altars, do you? We've mentioned music concerts and festivals. Folks, if the focus of an altar is not Jehovah God, then it is an evil altar; it is the altar of an idol. I like a sporting event from time to time. When the focus of the game goes from friendly competition to something that I've put a bet on, that is idolatry and that requires an altar. Anytime a sacrifice is done there must be an altar, or an altar was created by virtue of there having been a sacrifice. Money is a very common sacrifice and money altars are very common.

If I went to a sporting event, for example, but I didn't go there for the socialization of just being out and about with friends, and I didn't go there for the sport itself, but I went there to see and admire the quarterback, or the center, or the point guard--, whomever I think is the cutest, or the one I'd like to meet in real life, that is **idolatry**. That person either is an evil altar or I've turned them into one in my mind, or I would like to.

There's a thin line, folks. Careful.

I went to a wrestling match once and two women who sat behind us screamed out The Rock's name throughout... *as if.* This was in that dispensation of time when Dwayne Johnson had *become* The Rock, a wrestling phenomenon before he converted back to being Dwayne Johnson again. Those women either made The Rock, which he is not--- Jesus is The

Rock--, but anyway they had sought to make this human into an altar, or he already was one, or on his way to becoming one to himself, to them, or to the world.

And the *way* they called his name was not G-rated or God-approved. Yes, there are sex altars, and sex is worship; it is an altar all unto itself. People make sex into an idol, especially Madison Avenue; sex sells. Sex is used to sell pretty much everything.

The marriage bed is an altar; and it should be undefiled. The single person's bed can also be an altar if there is sexual activity going on in it---, any kind of sexual activity. Having sex alone, as in masturbation, is idolatry and it is offering worship to the altar of masturbation. That is an evil and dangerous, addictive altar. Every time you spill seed or exert sexual energy, even by yourself, you lose glory, you lose power, and you can be losing opportunities in the natural as well as money.

For those who live to eat, there are food altars, and food can be an altar. Jezebel's table, where the prophets who served her ate was an altar.

There are places where money is worshipped. A casino is an altar. A bingo hall can be an altar. Any type of buying or selling, unless God is the focal point and the reason for it being in place is a money altar.

Jesus turned over the money changers table that was in the temple.

Why?

It was an altar--, an altar competing with the altar of worship and sacrifice in the Temple. People--, especially carnal people find it easier to serve what they see more than what they do not see, so I'm sure that money altar got a lot of *play*.

> Jesus said to him, "Thomas, because you have seen Me, you have believed. Blessed are those who have not seen, and have yet believed." (John 20:29)

The Public Altar

I call an altar in public view a public altar while it may not be that at all, since there is a priest priesting over it. It's not like a BBQ grill at the park that you can just walk up to and use if no one else is using it. I'll just say that it is in plain view, as altars are supposed to be, anyway.

However, if you watch certain movies for example and there is a shrine, there is a man or woman who lives in the place where that shrine is--, they most likely created the shrine, or inherited it from the previous witchdoctor, shaman, or *whatever,* like it's a family business.

People come to see that person, the priest, priestess, oracle, witchdoctor, spirit healer, shaman—whatever one may call this person to get favors from demons. Well, that's not what they think they are doing. They believe they come there to solve problems--, they may not have given a thought as to <u>how</u> those problems will be solved, they just want them solved.

If the altar is not to Jehovah God, then it is to demons. Renaming demons *"the gods,"* only makes them idol *gods*, but they are still devils and demons. If the person gets relief of any kind, they will now owe that devil, demon, or idol god that "helped" them. They may have only traded one problem for another, and sometimes the new problem is far worse.

But we cannot, even in our country or our culture, surmise that an altar, even in plain view, is a Godly altar, because people migrate from and to all over the world; the world is a melting pot, these days.

While we all should have our own individual altar and a family altar, there comes a time of corporate worship, and we do not fail to assemble ourselves together. At that spot we worship and serve at a corporate altar—our church's altar.

I'd like to hear from the man or woman of God that says, like Abraham or Noah, God told that man to **build an altar**, not build a church. Yes, the personal and family altar in his own home--, but so many say that God told him to build a *church*. I've not heard anyone say that God told them to build an <u>*altar*</u>. We cannot presuppose that altar and church are synonymous; they are not.

Most who have been "called to build a church" have few to no comments or teachings about the altar of their church, and I'm not sure why that is. Mostly "the altar" is just used as a location where people come to either get saved, bring their money, or get prayed for by the elders of that congregation. You know--, the *altar call*.

But what kind of altar is at that church? How did it come to be? What did God say about that church's altar? He gave specific directions in the Bible how altars were to be built; God is very specific. How is your church's altar maintained? How is it serviced? How is that altar of that your church *priested* over? Is it sanctified? What happens if it is defiled?

I am in no way promoting making the church's altar an idol. We worship God but we need a proper and Godly altar to reach God. Again, the altar can be physical and or spiritual.

You can tell everything about a man or woman of God by how they acknowledge or ignore, respect or disrespect the Altar that they priest over.

Not focusing on the altar of a religious building but instead on the edifice that should surround the altar is the same as adorning oneself but not being concerned with one's health. Oh, I've seen many gorgeous people, dressed to the nine's—but their teeth need immediate support.

What did God tell a man, or a woman to build when He told them to build?

We weren't privy to their conversation with God but in their testimony, shall they not tell us? We know that God told Abraham to build an altar, as well we know many others in the Bible who were told by the Lord to build and altar to the Lord. These altars were places of memorial. They were places where God met man. They were places where God made covenant with man. They were memorials so that man or those people that that man led, such as Moses in the Wilderness, or a godly shepherd leading a congregation, would never forget what God had done for them and how God had revealed Himself a certain way at this certain spot.

Common Altars

If there are so many altars in the fields and groves, and high places, who told those people to build those altars? Need? Greed? Lust? Tradition? Superstition? Competition?— their neighbor has one? The devil told them to build those altars that are in the "high places."

Seems people are very adept at hearing from and obeying the devil, especially when he's telling them to do things that God has told them not to do.

God is speaking. God is still speaking; can't we hear Him? The devil is not the only one talking, folks. We should endeavor to hear God, rather than listening to the default in this Earth--, the devil.

Common altars were listed in a previous book, **Repent of Visiting Evil Altars,** so we will not relist the types here. This book is mostly about the church altar inside the building, and evaluating that, be it good or bad, Godly or evil.

The area of the church just in front of the pulpit is generally called the altar, but many churches do not have an altar anymore. In most people's mind then, an altar is a space. An altar is not a space, but the area where the altar should be, when there is no physical altar there is called the altar. More appropriately it should be called the altar area or the altar space.

Churches aren't designed as they once were. The need to have a place to worship may place people in homes, storefronts, tents, any number of places and it may not be expedient to build the exterior or the interior in classical church style. Plus, I hope we are realizing that it is the altar, where the physical world interfaces with the spiritual world that is most important and not the trappings around it, although God should have a beautiful "Tent of Meetings."

This book is not even about the physical altar of a church, your church—any church. It is about the **spiritual** altar of that church.

Now that you know what an evil altar is, compare it to the altar that you are attending as you visit from church to church or as you visit churches looking for a "church home." The spiritual altar is invisible, but you will know of that altar by the Fruit of that place. So, remain attentive.

God Loves a Good Altar

An altar of earth you shall make for me and sacrifice on it your burnt offerings and your peace offerings, your sheep and your oxen. In every place where I cause my name to be remembered I will come to you and bless you.
(Exodus 20:24)

The people in the Bible who obeyed God and built Godly altars are mentioned throughout the Old Testament. Noah built an altar, Abraham, Jacob, among others.

And Moses built an altar and called the name of it, The Lord Is My Banner,
(Exodus 17:15 ESV)

Elijah dealt with 450 prophets of Baal in a contest on Mount Carmel. There were only two altars there, one to Jehovah

God and one to Baal, but our God answered by fire. An altar with no fire is a weak altar.

Folks, sacrificing on an altar and calling on and invoking the name of and the presence of Jehovah is like throwing up a bat signal in the sky for Batman. While we don't compare the Only Living God to fictional idols, **God communes and communicates with His people through altars.** All the spirit world copies that and that is why there are evil altars. The only difference is the kingdom of darkness seems to know this consciously, while saved folks may not give it a thought. Saved folks may not even think about the altar while they are at church with their wallets and or purses open taking out a tithe, or a sacrifice, or an offering. Let me say that again, if you were leading a bull up to an altar on Mount Carmel, wouldn't you be very aware of what you were doing and why? Is taking money out of your wallet too easy for you to realize why you are placing it on a Godly altar? **It's a sacrifice.**

If you had a date with someone that you absolutely love and they told you the time and place to meet them, would you? If you don't know what they look like and they told you to bring a red rose so they could recognize you, would you? God says something like, *Meet me at the altar and bring a sacrifice, and I will meet you there.* Even if you go to church and you bring the sacrifice, but your attention and intention is not to press in and meet God at the time of the offering, have you really met God there? Or did you just go through some motions?

Maybe it is better to meet God at home, in a quiet place such as your prayer room. Perhaps there are too many distractions at church. However, the corporate altar is more powerful than your individual altar at home. Not only that, some spiritual matters cannot and should not be addressed alone--, you need the corporate anointing and power to handle some negative spiritual powers.

Kings & Altars

The kings of the Bible who either tore down and or erected Godly altars were praised and loved by the Lord.

You shall tear down their altars and dash in pieces their pillars and burn their Asherim with fire. You shall chop down the carved images of their gods and destroy their name out of that place. You shall not worship the Lord your God in that way. (Deuteronomy 12:3-4 ESV)

Those who did the opposite were hated by God; and most often they were removed. The kings who let altars be built and remain in groves and in high places all over the place were disparaged by God, as those unsanctioned altars were witchcraft or occultic in origin and nature.

Before the altar contest on Mount Carmel, Elijah had to repair the altar of the Lord that had been defiled, (1 Kings 18:30). In the Book of Ezra we also see the altar of the Lord being rebuilt:

> Then Jeshua son of Jehozadak joined his fellow priests and Zerubbabel son of Shealtiel with his family in rebuilding the altar of the God of Israel. They wanted to sacrifice burnt offerings on it, as instructed in the Law of Moses, the man of God. (Ezra 3:2)

> See, I have set you this day over nations and over kingdoms, to pluck up and to break down, to destroy and to overthrow, to build and to plant. (Jeremiah 1:10)

In Bible days the altar was always consulted before military actions, battles and wars. The altar was the connection to God that would ensure victory and often giving the entire battle plan ahead of the battle.

Gideon was instructed to tear down his father's altars. It is understood that a new altar is not built until the old, evil altar is torn down.

That night the Lord said to him, "Take your father's bull, and the second bull seven years old, and pull down the altar of Baal that your father has, and cut down the Asherah that is beside it and build an altar to the Lord your God on the top of the stronghold here, with stones laid in due order.

Then take the second bull and offer it as a burnt offering with the wood of the Asherah that you shall cut down." So Gideon took ten men of his servants and did as the Lord had told him.

But because he was too afraid of his family and the men of the town to do it by day, he did it by night. When the men of the town rose early in the morning, behold, the altar of Baal was broken down, and the Asherah beside it was cut down, and the second bull was offered on the altar that had been built.
(Jude 6:25-28 ESV)

God Hates an Evil Altar

God hates idolatry and therefore He hates an evil altar, and as you've seen in the last chapter, He gives explicit instructions that they should be torn down. In 1 Kings 13, God sent a young prophet to *cry against the evil altar* and decree that it would be torn down. God hates an evil altar, and why shouldn't He. The presence of that evil altar means that idolatry is going on--, the worship of some devil, demon, or idol *god*.

And behold, a man of God came out of
Judah by the word of the Lord to Bethel.
Jeroboam was standing by the altar to
make offerings. And the man cried
against the altar by the word of
the Lord and said, "O altar, altar, thus

says the Lord: 'Behold, a son shall be born to the house of David, Josiah by name, and he shall sacrifice on you the priests of the high places who make offerings on you, and human bones shall be burned on you.'" And he gave a sign the same day, saying, "This is the sign that the Lord has spoken:

'Behold, the altar shall be torn down, and the ashes that are on it shall be poured out.'"

And when the king heard the saying of the man of God, which he cried against the altar at Bethel, Jeroboam stretched out his hand from the altar, saying, "Seize him."

And his hand, which he stretched out against him, dried up, so that he could not draw it back to himself.

The altar also was torn down, and the ashes poured out from the altar, according to the sign that the man of God had given by the word of the Lord. (1 Kings 13:1-11)

While reading v.10 of the above passage I get the imagery of those loyal to Hitler stretching out their hands in allegiance and agreement to do evil, exclaiming, *Heil Hitler.* I can imagine those outstretched arms so rigid and intense that they can't draw them back again.

So, what type of altar are you serving or worshipping at these days? Pray, ask the Holy Spirit and also become a Fruit Inspector--, you shall know them by their *Fruit.* Evil fruit? No thank you. Some things we tolerate, some things we pray about, some things we shun and run away from. I am not trying to tell you what to do other than to open your spiritual eyes and use your discernment, pray to the Lord and listen to the Holy Spirit regarding what altar you are working with right now.

If you've been faithful and sowing for years and years at the altar that you are at and nothing seems to be happening, then you ask God about that. Yes, we look at ourselves and walk upright before the Lord, following the disciplines of the faith. None of us are perfect, but could the altar that you are submitted to be the problem?

How did you happen to pick that church anyway? Really you chose the altar, not so much the church, although you may *think* you chose the church. How did you choose that altar, anyway? Mom and Dad and Grandma went here? You like the music? You like the preacher; he's funny? Your friends go there? That's nice.

- Can you meet and interface with God at that altar?
- Do your prayers get answered?
- Does corporate prayer get answered in that place?
- You're saved, yes; but how are the other factors of your salvation faring there?
- How's your conversion to a son of God coming along?
- Are you compelled to convert to be more Christ like?

- Are you encouraged by the leadership and helped by the Holy Ghost to do the same?

If your answers are positive, then it seems God is in that place.

Folks, you can't judge that God is in a place just because there are signs and wonders and miracles. The devil can do that stuff. Pharoah's' magicians had snake tricks in the palace. The move of God is not necessarily so because you felt emotional, happy, sad, or cried. Was that God? Was that God that moved you?

What *spirit* interfaced with the local congregation that you sat in while you were at "church" last week? You have to discern every *spirit*--- ***every spirit***, even at "church."

Kings & Priests

Some kings were also priests. Some kings were only kings, and they were not supposed to be doing any priestly duties. Those who disobeyed God regretted it.

The priests came from the Levites and God appointed them. Nowhere did I find in my Bible a priest trying to usurp or consolidate power to become king. That is kind of mindboggling because in today's celebrity pastor and celebrity prophet world those who are, and hopefully called to be priests have made themselves into kings. The congregation is guilty of supporting this, but many congregations have been bewitched. I've been in such a congregation where the people are almost like cut outs, they do whatever the pastor says, blindly and don't even realize they are under a spell.

A king, even a king was not to bypass, or overstep the priesthood, the priestly authority of the priest who solidly hears from God. Saul was one such king who performed priestly duties instead of waiting for Samuel. God cut off Saul from that very day.

Melchizedek, the King of Salem was already a priest and a king, so he was not violating anything that God had put in place. We who are in Christ are called to be priests, but we are also *little k kings* in the Earth as the Lord is the King of kings—that's us.

> And it is yet far more evident: for that after the similitude of Melchisedec there ariseth another priest, Who is made, not after the law of a carnal commandment, but after the power of an endless life. For he testifieth, Thou art a priest for ever after the order of Melchisedec.
> (Hebrews 7:15-17)

Yes, we are called to be priests, and we are *little k kings* in the Earth; we are being trained to reign, but we stay in our lane, the lane that God has planned for each of us. The fear of the Lord is the beginning of Wisdom; keep respecting God, and live.

Priesting At an Altar

How do you expect to get something different from an altar than the altar is?

How do you expect to get anything different from an altar than the type of priest you have priesting at that altar?

The author of Hebrews declares the priesthood of Melchizedek to be far superior to the Levitical order. Melchizedek obviously was a higher and greater altar than Abraham since Abraham *tithed* to Him. Could this be why there are so few who tithe? They either have a wrong relationship with Mammon, or they don't know what an altar is. Or, could it be that they don't see the altar where they are as a greater altar than they themselves? The altar at the church they attend is not a greater altar to them than the mall?

Do we subliminally not want Jesus to receive or accept our sacrifices? Do we not believe that our sacrifices are good enough? Do we know they are inferior? Are we avoiding Jesus, but we like "church" because our friends are there and it's a fun time?

Let's say the altar that you visit weekly, or biweekly **is** a Godly altar. Are you sacrificing on that altar? This is especially important because, hopefully not in that same church building, but somewhere, maybe in a grove, a *high place*, or in a shrine, an evil priest may be sacrificing against you, your life, your marriage, money, career, family or destiny.

What are you doing to counter this? Anything?

If Elijah could come up against 450 evil prophets in a sacrifice contest, that should give us a clue as to the power we wield in sacrificing on a Godly altar. Rephrasing: Evil sacrifices against you must be countered not just by having a higher, better, greater, and more powerful altar, but using it with proper sacrifices on it that get God's attention.

How is the altar at your church maintained as a Godly altar? What will corrupt and pollute it? A defiled offering. A defiled priest.

What good is it then? How is that altar redeemed, or does it have to be destroyed and rebuilt?

They say that whoever we sit under we will receive of their grace. Add to that, whoever is priesting at the altar that we are praying at, worshipping at, or sacrificing at will determine, or at least have impact on how that altar will connect us to God and how that altar will serve us.

Just as God approved some kings and Israel fared well under them, but God's people did not fare well under evil and idolatrous kings, the same is true of the priest of the church you attend.

Recall, there could be hundreds of walking altars coming into the church on any given Sunday, so the corporate or Church altar has to be for real. This is why the pastor, and the praise minister beg for **unity** every service. God commands the blessing where there is unity.

But it is also why the pastor and all those who priest at the altar of your church have to have pure hearts and clean hands, else, they can defile the altar. Whatever they are, whatever their *spiritual* status is, the congregation will eventually become unless they recognize the corruption and have a proper prayer life and altar of their own.

By the same token, the persons attending that church and making use of the altar have to have Godly lifestyle for that altar to work for them. Recall the laver basin.

Family Altar, Family Priest

The anointing flows from the top. Do you *priest* at an altar or do you attend that altar, or do *you* service that altar? Whatever you are, spiritually, the people you priest over, will become that. The same is true in the House of God, so you have to be wise as to who ministers to you, speaks over your life, lays hands on you, and prays for you.

Whether you are the principal priest over an altar, or you are a participant in a corporate altar, do you empower and enable that altar with your own sacrifices? Are you using the altar, or is the altar using *you*--, or **both**?

One of the main people to look at is the pastor. Pray hard about this because he is the main priest of that house. Look at the people he most intimately priests to, his wife, his children--, his family.

Are they all put together, or are they a hot mess? Are they genuine, or are they fake? Do they exhibit Fruit of the Spirit of God, or fruit of some other *spirit*? Are the kids normal or are they spoiled brats? Is there favoritism or is everyone treated well? What those kids are or have become is a result of how this man *priests* his home. Will he be able to priest over the altar of that church better than he priests at home with one wife and two kids and a dog? At church there are 300 of you, 500, 3,000 of you—will he be able to priest better over 3,000 than he can over 4?

You know that answer.

I used to be of the mindset that God's got His eye on the pastor, so I don't really need to worry about it. But, I've changed my mind on that because that pastor is the main priest, priesting over the altar that is connecting me in the physical world to God in the spiritual world in corporate services. We pray for our leadership, both spiritual and civil. But I don't need to look at either in judgment as if I want to do something to them; God's got that.

Since Jesus tore the veil between man and God, we don't need a priest to connect us to God, but in corporate settings such as the church we attend, there is a shepherd who is to be respected in that position, and he does minister at or over the altar of that church.

Can this man reach God? Does he talk to God? Does he hear and listen to God? Is he faithful to say what thus saith the Lord, and not something made up? Is he courageous enough to say what thus saith the Lord when it is something that will not be popular with the crowd?

I am not asking if this man is perfect; I want to know is he dedicated to his priesthood. That is important because it concerns me and my entire family, and our futures because this is the Altar that I have chosen for us to both worship at and make sacrifices unto the Lord. Even if I have an altar at home, at some point my physical offerings and sacrifices must be made to a higher altar than my home altar. At some point we bring all the tithes into the storehouse as in Malachi 3:10.

Don't rivers flow into bigger rivers, and eventually into the ocean?

Will my sacrifices make it to the Lord? Like the priest that went into the Holy of Holies once a year with a rope tied around his foot, if this man gets into the Holy of Holies, will he walk out by his own two legs, or will he have to be dragged out, by that rope--, dead?

Ultimately, I ask, *Will the favor and the answers to my sacrifices from the Lord ever reach me through this altar?*

Forgetfulness

Man has a tendency to forget. Since all the ways of a man are clean in his own eyes, man especially forgets the wrongs that he has done. So even if a man, especially a parent forgets all of their past wrongs--, sins, crimes, missteps, and mistakes as they vow to do better, to do right, or suddenly want to set a good example for their own children, they may forget the sins of their own youth. They may forget the sins they committed yesterday--, just yesterday. Some people think just stopping a behavior is all that is needed to make all the issues that go with that sinful behavior also stop and go away.

A man smokes for 30 years and then he stops, cold turkey. Are all the damages of smoking for 3 decades suddenly reversed? *If only...*

Nope.

Because of the sin and sinful behavior, covenants were made--, evil covenants. Those covenants were made in blood. God doesn't look too kindly on breaking covenants, and how do you as a human, in your flesh expect to stop a demon that is coming to enforce a curse that is the result of an evil covenant that may have a *forever* clause in it, that was made in blood?

If you stop the behavior that keeps the demon in your life that doesn't mean they will go immediately away without deliverance; that's what I mean by you exerting your flesh over a spiritual *thing*. By stopping, using sheer will power, that's good, but it is only flesh.

They may just hang around hoping for another opportunity with you. They may just hang around even if you haven't stopped; so you think they are gone. They may just hide to ambush you later.

You can't stop a speeding train by standing on the railroad tracks by will power, just because you **want** the train to stop. Nope, that train won't stop unless the conductor sees you, wants to stop, has time to stop, and can stop.

Evil covenants are in place because of evil altars. If the evil altar is being priested over, then the evil covenant persists. If there is an evil covenant, then there are also curses that are being enforced against you. It all spawns from the altar.

- What altar are you serving, servicing, or offering sacrifices and worship on?
- What ancestor, connected to you by blood carried your name to an evil altar?

- What spiritual authority put your name by spiritual connection on an evil altar?
- What evil altar did you unwittingly just walk to on your own and sit under for months and years, and also take one or more sacrifices there, saying I accept, I agree, I join to this *altar*?
- What demons, devils, or idols have you let into your life, knowingly or unknowingly by being joined to a certain altar?

To answer that, look at who is priesting over that altar; they are first partakers of the good or bad from that altar. Does the priest of the altar that you are at look like someone you want to be *like*? Would you want your children to be like the person priesting over the altar whose spiritual influence you are sitting under?

Whatever *spirits* are connected to that altar—here they come into your life.

Oh, make it stop!

Sometimes that is our cry to the Lord, *Make it stop.*

However, a demon doesn't have any desire to stop, as long as you are connected to that altar, and especially worshipping at it and sacrificing on it, whatever evil *spirits* connected to that altar are now connected to you.

Yes, we know we should be connected to and connecting to the Holy Spirit, but here we are speaking of evil, false, fake, and probably occult (hidden) altars.

Demons don't stop until they are **made** to stop. They have to be **made** to stop and that must happen by a GREATER altar.

That will take Jesus Christ, the greatest altar, spiritual warfare, the Blood of Jesus, and combinations of warfare verbiage, decrees, declarations, repentance, renunciation, denunciations, fasting, deliverance, and et cetera. It's doable, but it can get complicated.

Oh, saints of God, it is so much easier to walk circumspectly and never enter into evil covenants. But there is no condemnation here, we all have sinned and fallen short of the Glory of God.

This ancestor of yours may forgive themselves and consider all the wrong they did forgotten and over with. **It's not.** The blood that they made one or more evil covenants with is still speaking. The blood on the altar is still speaking, and that's why the altar is still emanating against your bloodline. Your parents may feel relief, **but it is still in there--, waiting. Waiting for opportunity.**

The virus that makes a person have a cold takes 2 to 3 days to incubate. The virus is in there on Monday, but if the immune system doesn't rise up to defeat it, by Thursday someone will be blowing their nose.

Spiritual warfare is as the immune response to get what is already acting out, or is in you and your bloodline, incubating, waiting to attack you, out of your system for good. Else, it's only a matter of time. Covenants are certainly all about time. Always.

Spiritual warfare is us calling on the Lord, asking Him to arise and contend with those who are contending with us. (Psalm 35:1)

Your parents and ancestors may mean well and may do all that forgiving but forget to repent. This is the *why* of this book. We must always repent, and we must also repent for our parents and our ancestors. We have that authority and that responsibility.

Repentance can be, *Lord, forgive me for all my sins, forgive me for sins of omission and commission, in the Name of Jesus.*

Or, more thoroughly we can repent for everything--, line upon line, and sin upon sin. In my humble opinion, as detailed as you can be in your repentance regarding visiting evil altars, the sooner you will put the entire sin and iniquity to rest, in the Name of Jesus.

Visiting an evil altar is more than just going to some physical structure and requesting that a demon do something for you. As said, the altar can come to you. Also, in the list of the types of altars, the altar may not even be physical, but spiritual. Let's say, and we pray this is not so, that one of your ancestors decided to kill someone, or some other heinous sin. So, they formulated a plan and did that. They may not have even been saved; they may not have seen what they did as a sin, but only as a crime since they were a good citizen before they did this act.

Now, instead of repenting, they worked for the rest of their lives to cover it up. Maybe in the physical world they didn't get found out, but all the paperwork and requisite iniquity was posted to the foundation of your bloodline. Nobody in your immediate family way back all those generations or forward from that time ever knew about this bloodshed, but there is iniquity and debt to pay for it. *Tag--*, you may be *it*. We pray not and we pray it out of the foundation and out of your life, in the Name of Jesus, **Amen.**

Look at this, they didn't, as far as they know, go to any altar, but they did. To get the idea to commit a sin, any sin, even murder, means **evil** came to the ancestor or the ancestor sought out the evil. To formulate the plan one or more demons were invoked. To figure out how to get away with it, same or different demons were employed. All sin is demon-inspired; all sin is anointed and devil-assisted. If you sin, an evil covenant was made and ratified. When you sin, you owe the devil who assisted you. Without repentance and forgiveness, this evil covenant usually spans generations, and has to be broken.

How do you know any of this happened in your bloodline? Pray; ask the Holy Spirit after you notice that things are not going well in your own life. Such as? Well, for an example, every time you start something good, some how it dies or gets killed and never lives. That *spirit of murder* may have been released into your bloodline when your great-great *somebody* did something that was not so great--, like murder or shed innocent blood. You or someone in your bloodline may have homicidal rage even at the slightest provocation. There may be a spirit of murder in that family's foundation.

Another way to know that you have serious foundation problems that need to be addressed is you keep picking bad pastors, false teachers, evil prophets, and wrong churches.

All that boils down to wrong altars. I know of a person, try as they may in prayer and fasting, is attracted to ALL the wrong stuff that a person can be attracted to. No, I'm not talking about sin, but this person is attracted to down low occultic teachers, preachers and pastors. This person is attracted to witchcraft and diviners. This person is attracted to everything evil that works against their life and try to use them (usually for money) who are all masquerading in churches or under the guise of being *of* God. This person has zero discernment, most likely because of not having the real Holy Spirit, but evil *spirits* masquerading as the Holy Spirit, when they are not and cannot ever be Him.

By this deception and possibly by markers in their blood, this person is drawn to fake altars, fake everything. All the while, they are desperately fasting and praying and making no progress in life. When they meet someone who can tell them any of this, they are immediately drawn away by the *familiar spirits* in the people that they idolize and spend way too much time with and attention on.

Pray, saints of God if you know such a person. In time, perhaps they will let God help them before it's too late.

Fake Churches

There are plenty of folks that make their living and make it their business to blow the whistle on churches or pastors that they believe are fakes. I'm not called to do that.

There are also evil altars at fake churches. How can you tell if a church is fake? Ask God. There are false pastors, false prophets aplenty. If the altar at your church is not a proper interface to the Spirit of God, then you will need to pray diligently so the Holy Spirit can advise you.

Trusting that every building with a steeple or a cross on it or in it is of God and has been planted by God, is sanctioned and ordained by God is a big jump.

There are so many dangers in a fake church and at an evil altar. What you may have been initiated into or what may have been taken from you or transferred from you at a false altar is for the Lord to reveal to you through His Holy Spirit. The purpose of a false altar is to deceive you, initiate you, steal from you, possibly even kill or destroy you, possibly use you the sacrifice to satisfy some requirement or desire of the demon who is exerting power and influence over the "person" who is priesting at the evil altar.

Lord, forbid, in the Name of Jesus.

Stay prayed up folks, people have their motives.

Hopefully, you, your parents or your ancestors didn't go there knowingly, but the spiritual fallout from having gone to that evil or fake altar, agreed with that altar, given offerings of money, worship, or time on that altar still constituted an evil covenant. That evil covenant allows demons into your life and into the lives of your family.

Remember, covenants are made and forged in blood and unless they are broken with their associated curses, they will continue on into the generations.

Be sure to repent for your own mistakes and sins, as well as those of your parents and ancestors.

Deceived Churches

I've heard at least one pastor say that people come to church for the fellowship and stay for the relationships. That's nice, if it's a social club.

You'd better come to a church for the altar because people are people and when people are behaving just like the folks that they are, will that altar be working for you? Will the altar at that church still be interfacing you with God and the physical with the spiritual world? – Especially in your time of need? Yes, you have your individual or home altar, but the corporate altar wields a mightier power and greater spiritual influence.

When you go into that building, or even when you are not in that building can you reach God because of the offerings and sacrifices that are on that particular altar that is supposed to be serving you? Can you rely on the corporate altar that man or woman of God is priesting at to enable spiritual transactions that you need to make to work for you? Here, I speak of offerings as a spiritual transaction.

> He saw in a vision evidently about the ninth hour of the day an angel of God coming in to him, and saying unto him, Cornelius.
> And when he looked on him, he was afraid, and said, What is it, Lord? And he said unto him, Thy prayers and thine alms are come up for a memorial before God. (Acts 10:3-4)

Your offerings that you placed on the corporate altar of your church were to have been accepted, blessed by the set man of your church and received by the Lord.

If your offerings didn't go to God, then how will God **remember** them when He wants to bless you or when you want

Him to bless you? If your offerings didn't make it to God, then where did they go? Who took them, spiritually speaking? If you do not see 30-, 60-, or 100-fold return in your offerings, that's kind of a clue that God wasn't involved in the transaction. Through the altar at the church you attend and give at, are you receiving any type of return on your sacrificial offerings?

Huh--, better pray and ask God.

When I refer to an altar as being witchy, or dark, hidden, or occultic as an evil altar, I must say that you could be at a church that seems like a great place but if there is NO POWER from the altar, what good is it to you? If that altar cannot protect you or fight for you, and win spiritual battles for you, why do you think that is? It is most likely that that particular altar is NOT greater than another altar that is working in your life. Are you servicing an ungodly altar yourself, on the down low?

Stop it! Renounce the worship at an ungodly altar. This is the epitome of doublemindedness if you go to a church, but you regularly service another sinful altar that you think no one knows about. A doubleminded man will receive nothing from God.

It could be that your church's altar is a Godly altar but it is cold because **you** are not working it, or **you** are in sin and not repenting, and there may be multiple evil altars working against your life.

You've been a faithful member and you've been going to the same church for so many years--, a decade even. Provided that you are not an undercover sinner, what has your connection with that church done for you? What has that altar done for you? Has that altar fought for you, providing you spoke to the altar in faith and with expectation to fight for you? Have you been faithful to keep that altar burning with proper disciplines, including sacrifices?

Job offered up sacrifices regularly before the devil attacked him viciously, and the devil still was able to attack him.

Saints of God, if Job didn't have sacrifices in memorial, as the Word says that Cornelius' offerings had come up as a memorial to him, how long do you think Job's ordeal would have lasted? How do you think Job's testing would have turned out?

So, if you are going to a church, a building, an altar then stay for your **relationship** with that altar, more so than staying there just because you like the people. The people part of a church relationship is important and can determine if one wants to stay or go, but that altar. When you find the right altar and that altar is working spiritual matters out for you, somehow you will find the will to love everyone in that congregation.

But when the altar is not working, God may be leading you away from that church because He has a better and correct fit for you. When the altar is not working for you, you are most likely grumpy yourself, and the people may not even like you, not to mention you looking sideways at the people.

We may be crying out for the pastor to pray for us, the elders, the intercessors—and the Bible does say that. But the altar and the sacrifices on that altar are interfacing with the spiritual realm to fight for you. You do have a regular and proper sacrifice on that altar, *yes*?

The stronger OF TWO ALTARS WILL WIN SPIRITUAL BATTLES. Altars are strengthened, yes in praise and worship and prayer and the Word, and with sacrifices.

The Israelites kept sacrifices on their Godly altars burning 24/7. Why do you think that is? For strength. For power. Those sacrifices please GOD and when God is pleased, He arises and comes to your situation.

You don't believe me? Huh. When you are at a ball game and some player makes an exceptional play, what is the first thing you do? You get up out of your seat; you arise.

When you are at a concert, albeit secular, and the musician plays extremely well, so well it kinda goes through you, what do you do? You get up out of your seat, sometimes in amazement, sometimes in disbelief, but most often because you are impressed. You stand up; you arise.

When the concert or the program is over and you are duly impressed, what do you do? You give a standing ovation. You stand, you get up, you arise.

When you are in a church, a church with liberty, and the Word is coming forth and it is speaking to your spirit man, what do you do? You get up out of your seat, off that pew. Your spirit man stands up, therefore your physical person stands up; you arise.

God is resting from Creation. Jesus is seated at the Right Hand of the Father. This is why we pray and cry out, O, God arise. Yes, God will hear our cries when we pray fervently and ask Him to arise, but without saying a word, when our offerings and our sacrifices impress God-

-, when they please Him—that is the same as an exceptional play and He will arise and come to you and your situation. It's as though God is saying, *Look at that one, look at that play.* ***Look at that sacrifice. That one gets it. Wow!***

Before sin, before The Fall in the Garden of Eden, God came down in the cool of the day to commune with Adam and Eve. Those two were doing what they were supposed to be doing, dressing the Garden. They hadn't learned to sin yet, so God was impressed. Their stewardship over the Garden was their worship, it was their offering, it was their sacrifice; they impressed God, so He AROSE and came down, *regularly*.

Cain and Abel brought their sacrifices to God. The Bible indicates that God was approving of Abel's, but not Cain's. To me, that may mean that God was where Abel was because I kinda think He got up because **that offering pleased Him**. While He was there, He heard Abel's blood crying out from the ground and asked Cain where was his brother? Abel's offering brought God to his *situation* a*nd while there, God could hear Abel's blood crying out.*

When God arises and comes to your situation because of your proper sacrifices on a proper altar, He will definitely hear your prayers and requests. God answers our prayers while we are yet praying, as well the answers are Yes and Amen.

When you offer good hospitality don't people keep coming back to your house? When a restaurant, for example, has a good reputation, when the *fame* of that restaurant goes out, people will arise and come there. The restaurant has good *offerings* on their menu. Good offerings draw people, even God.

It's not a restaurant but evaluate if the altar of your church is *feeding* you properly.

A Good Altar Is Hard to Find

Is worship and the Presence of God possible at the church you are going to? I was in a church once where in more than a year I was able to enter into worship only once. Was it an altar problem or a choir problem, I don't know. Was it me? Nope. I could enter into worship at home, even in my car on the way, I could enter into worship with other churches' on television or even online, but not at that particular "altar."

Are you really worshipping, or just having fun, jumping and dancing, calling it praise, and having a good time?

When was the last time you were able to enter into worship either alone or with the praise team or the worship minister at your church?

Why aren't your offerings working according to Scripture? Could be the altar you are working with.

Why can't you see God? Could be the altar.

Hear God? Could it be the altar?

Reach God? Maybe it's the altar.

Israelites lost the Ark of the Covenant to the Philistines who had defeated them in war. The enemies of God stole the Ark of the Covenant from the Israelites. Why would they do that? Because it was the source of their power; they did it to defeat them in battle. While the Ark of the Covenant was in the possession of the Philistines they suffered greatly. They suffered plagues and other disasters, so they wanted to get this item out of their possession and back into the hands of the Israelites.

The Ark of the Covenant is an altar; the highest altar of the Old Testament. People who are at the wrong altar will suffer; the Philistines suffered. People who abuse the altar suffer; Uzzah touched the Ark because he thought it would tilt and fall off the cart it was on. Even though it may have seemed like an innocent touch, Uzzah died. Mishandling an altar can be devastating, disappointing, and even deadly when it is not *your* altar.

Altars are very powerful.

While the Ark of the covenant was captured, the Israelites suffered as well. Losing the Ark of the Covenant of losing the altar is huge. The prophet, Samuel exhorted the people to repent to God for this heinous loss. Obviously, this loss was due to sin.

Intending to go to a Godly altar but ending up at a fake altar, a false altar or an ungodly, evil altar is not beneficial to any aspect of your life and it may ruin or take a person's life. Not only that, generational issues may result because of attending to or serving a false altar without repentance.

1. Lord, I repent for my sins, the sins of my parents and my ancestors going back to Adam and Eve, where I retrieve my glory and my essence, in the Name of Jesus.

2. Lord, for every evil altar, every fake altar, every wrong and ungodly altar that I have contributed to, sacrificed on, or given to, Blood of Jesus cover me, and Lord I demolish and tear down that evil altar with the Thunder Hammer of God, in the Name of Jesus.

3. LORD, I remove my sacrifice from that ungodly altar by the power in the Blood of Jesus, in the Name of Jesus.

4. Blood of Jesus, cover me for this sin and ignorance and remove all iniquity from working against me, in the Name of Jesus.

Does your church's altar support interface with the Spirit of God? Does the man *priesting* at the altar *actually* worship, or does he sit there looking cool? Does he pray, or is he just telling everyone else what to do? Does he enter into the Holy of Holies? *Can* he enter into the Holy of Holies, and can he lead me and others there?

Does the praise minister go into the Holy of Holies? Can he lead me and others there, or is he just singing and putting on a show?

Somebody better hear this.

A Priest Forever

You are a priest forever in the order of Melchizedek (Psalm 110:4b)

Melchizedek, the King of Salem is a foreshadowing of Jesus. Melchizedek is described as being without ancestry, without beginning of days or end of life, (Hebrews 7). This writer believes that Melchizedek is a vision of Christ pre-incarnate, without earthly father, mother, or ancestry, without beginning of days or end of life. This could only be the Lord!

This brings clarity to why Abraham paid tithes to Him. The text says that Melchizedek as made to *resemble* Christ, so, he was a *type* or prefigurate of Christ.

There are types and shadows of Christ all through the Old Testament, but there are certain appearances in the OT, that I believe are Christ, Himself.

This writer also believes that the appearance of Melchizedek and Abraham's paying tithes to him is a parenthetical vision, like many in the Book of Revelation. I believe that what it is a vision of is Abraham paying tithes, 10% of all and the vision of that altar that Abraham established, interfacing the natural with the spiritual realm. Abraham's sacrifice was not only received in the Spirit, the image of Christ, as the King of Salem came down personally and accepted it. The Bible shows us this transaction in the Spirit, in words. **Abraham paying that tithe was so impressive and such a strong act of faith, saying LORD, You are real and I know it. It was so moving to God that Melchizedek came down in person to receive it.** The King of Salem, the King of Peace is Jesus Christ: HE AROSE.

Jesus is our Great Intercessor. He receives our sacrifices and uses them to worship the Father on our behalf.

Abraham had gotten the money (spoils) from doing battle with five kings to rescue his nephew, Lot. That was money out of the world, and it needed to be sanctified. Abraham sanctified it with fire, Holy Fire. Did Abraham have any more wars after he paid this tithe?

The Lord will reprove kings for your sake. Five kings were defeated in battle for the man of faith, Abraham.

Afterward Abraham sanctified the money he got, but he also paid it to the King of Salem, and *Salem* means *peace*. Look at Abraham's love for and dedication to Lot, that he would go to war for him, that he would fight five kings for him, and then give of the spoils, that is pay money for Lot. We can see God in all this and that the ransom He gave for us, even after all the fighting and battling was Jesus Christ. Amen.

The author of Hebrews declares this priesthood to be far superior to the Levitical order because Melchizedek obviously was a higher and greater altar than Abraham since Abraham ***tithed*** to Him. Could this be why so few tithe? They either have a wrong relationship with Mammon, or they don't know what an altar is. Or, could it be that they don't see the altar where they are as a greater altar than they themselves? The altar at the church they attend is not a greater altar to them than the mall? Then why are they there? For appearances? To socialize? *Why* are they there?

Are they there for the *show*? Just because a place or an event was miraculous and spiritual, doesn't make it of God. You do have to judge what is coming from that altar.

Are people living or dying in that place? If they are dying, then that is a dead church. A dead church has a dead or dormant altar.

Are babies being born to the members of that congregation? If not, then that is a dead church. A dead church has a missing, dormant, or dead altar, or it is not being priested over properly.

This is where I was last Spring--, asking the question, Do the sacrifices I put on the altar *multiply*? Do they return to me, some 30-, some 60- and some 100-fold as it says in the Gospels? In all honesty, that is what I was checking for. If you look over the history of the sacrifices you've placed on your church's altar, what is the net outcome? This is providing that you are sacrificing. I'm not talking about giving--, just giving even though the Word says that **with the same measure you give**, it shall be given back to you, pressed down, shaken together, and running over. So, if you give a dollar in the offering, you get a pressed-down, shaken together dollar back. Or, in some cases a few dollars running over. If the altar is not working, you may just get your dollar back. In some cases, you may get nothing back. Worse, that sacrifice can be spiritually misused and more money or other things you need for life and godliness can be taken from you.

Have you taken note of any returns of your **sacrifices**? Maybe it's not the altar, maybe it's the measure in which you are giving. God liked Abel's sacrifice, but not Cain's. *Just saying.*

Granted, none of us are perfect so we may not meet the criteria, or all the criteria of the 100-fold, or even 60-fold return, but can you take note of anything? Is the altar at your church working for you? Is it working for anyone?

The pastor. Oh, he dresses well, lives in a nice house and drives fine cars? And has an airplane? *Do tell.* But is the altar working for the congregation, the entire congregation, or the predominance of it? When you see one person in a place--, a family, a business, even a church prospering and nobody else is --, that is not God. Or are we to believe the pastor is the only one living upright before the Lord, and all the congregation is sinning at will, blocking their own blessings?

Hmmm.

How about in a family? I would suspect some occultic foul play actually if only one is prospering and the rest of the family is poor. At least, that is how I would direct my prayers.

Returns from a Godly altar is not money-for-money all the time. God will do so much more for your sacrifices, but you must hear God and know that the altar is a Godly altar. If you can't hear God, then look at your "returns" and see if they can be identified by what a Godly return should be by Scripture.

When I sacrificed every day in the month of March, God returned so many spiritual blessings to me, that ultimately saved my life. These returns were far more valuable than what money could buy.

Deceived People

Blind faith—don't do it unless God says so, and you know that you know that you heard it from God. Just because the pastor said so doesn't make it true and it doesn't make it the right thing for you to do.

Still, we pray for those that have authority over us, that means civil authority as well as spiritual authority. We pray for protection and coverage for our pastors and their family. We pray for clear Words from the Lord and that the *spirit of error* be bound and cast out of their lives and their ministry. We pray that they will minister and priest at the Altar of God in the edifice where they pastor or minister without *error*, in the Name of Jesus.

We should pray for our altars, yes, our home altars, as we sanctify it and put it into service, but also as we keep it in service using it daily, or at whatever intervals we use it.

Daily is best.

If we can cry out against an altar, as the Lord instructed the young prophet in 1 Kings 13, then we should also be able to cry out in support of a Godly altar to keep it running in top condition. If the altar is faulty, the people will receive *error* and be in error and may even fail and fall. The altar is the interface between the spiritual world and the physical world and if what we get is not true the people can be deceived and fall into collective captivity, other bondage, or worse.

- Altar, Altar, minister the Word of the Lord to me, in the Name of Jesus.
- Altar, Altar, receive my sacrifices in Spirit and in Truth and translate them to the Father that He may be glorified, in the Name of Jesus.

Judge an Altar

You shall know them by their fruit is not just for people, even though it is true of all people.

What comes out of an altar?

What comes out of the altar that you attend?

A dead altar is an ineffective altar. Look who's *priesting* at the altar. Are they getting the results that God says we all should get? It flows from the head, you know. Many of us think we are following successful people, proper leaders when we sometimes, and unfortunately become respecters of persons. If a leader *looks* successful and prosperous, man may flock to that person. They may have the ***look*** of prosperity, but are they *really*?

What are they like? Is their spouse happy? The best way to judge a man (not for judgment, but for evaluation) is to look at his wife. How does she look? Is she happy? You know it flows from the head.

Are there families in that congregation? How are they doing? Are there singles in the congregation; are they well-adjusted or buck wild, being forced to come to church out of guilt? Are there men as well as women in the congregation? This gets tricky because many churches have more women than men, but is it glaring? Are there 10% men to 90% women? Are the women married, or are they all single, smiling at the pastor, and dressed like *hoochie mammas*? The pastor likes *that*? Then what kind of *priesting* is he doing at that corporate altar?

Don't play.

Don't stay where they play; this is your real life. Ending up broke financially or broken spiritually because the priest of the house is a joker is not as bad as ending up in hell. *Playing*, player, down low, undercover, occultic and generally sinning "priests" lead whole congregations to the pit of hell. **Don't stay where they play with God and the things of the Spirit.**

Are the children in the congregation prospering? Look at the Fruit of that place. What is happening to the people who come in there or what has happened to those who have sat under this particular leadership and altar.

It all flows from the head.

Are these people prospering? Is anyone getting 30-, 60-, or 100-fold return on offerings, like EVER? It's not all about money, but if the Bible says that should be happening, then nothing should be able to stop it from happening--, except for sin, chronic, unrepented sin.

The answers to all these questions are very telling.

As it goes with evil altars, does anything go in that "church," are people carnal, in sin, doing whatever, and no one corrects them ever, either in the pews or from the pulpit?

Pulpit is a raised platform in Christian churches. It is not *pulp it,* meaning to take the solid out of a slurry, leaving only liquid. Pulp, as in fiction, is just a bunch of lies; please don't sit under that. You plan to change that? *How*? Only God can change this, but until He does, <u>it will change you</u> and that for the worse. Only God can correct a lying altar, a silly priest, buffooning over what should be God's altar.

Occultic, Undercover Altar

> Son of man cry against that altar.
> (1 Kings 13)

For those who decorate and love décor, you know that each room generally has one focal point.

A church should have its altar; let that be the focal point. The church should have **one altar**. The choir is not the focal point. The praise team or the music ministers are not to be the focal point. The dance ministry is not the focal point--, don't get me started on that. Anyway, neither the pastor nor his wife's hat should be the focal point. The Godly altar of that church is the focal point as it represents the spiritual altar that connects us to the spiritual realm of God.

Do people even build altars in a church anymore? They should. There is one man who changed the altar situation in a church and that man was Jesus. Jesus was a *sent* man, sent of God always. So when Jesus overturned the money tables in the synagogue He destroyed an altar that was competing with the altar that was already in the temple He attended. Jesus didn't pray over it and consecrate it to Godly use. Nope, He turned it over, disrupted it, destroyed its operation in the church. If it could have been corrected and "blessed," Jesus would have done that.

Forever in the state of Virginia, a dental office is a dental office, only, and it cannot also be something else at the same time. Forever it is that a church is supposed to be a church, built on the Revelation that Jesus is the Christ, and it shouldn't be anything else.

So, money changers: Get out of the Church. By money changers I also mean *hirelings* who are there for the collections, the money, the fame, the **perks**. Wolves who are on assignment of the devil or have assigned themselves as "pastors," you are the same as the money changers from the Bible, get out and leave God's people alone.

Careful, saints of God. You need to be saved and Spirit-filled to even go to some of these churches these days. Whole armor--,it's sad when you have to put on the whole armor of God to go into what is supposed to be a church. Especially after seeing the hidden occultism of some so-called churches and some pastors, you really want to run far away, as fast as possible in the other direction.

There are occultic pastors who get their powers for signs and wonders and miracles straight from hell. There are false pastors who get powers from the evil marine kingdom and through other demonic sources. Those people are hiding an occultic altar that they are actually servicing, and fronting that the "church" has a regular altar. When you have two competing altars, the greater altar will win every time. The only problem is when the one who is priesting over the trusting people of a congregation, the altar that is getting the most worship and sacrifices will win.

Yes, it is as bad as the occultic person is in the church for his or her gain, only. The absolute worst is when the people believe they are at one altar, but it is only a façade, and they don't even know they are worshipping another whole, demonic altar. Folks, you are worshipping the same altar your "priest" is worshipping at. If he or she is speaking into your life, there is a very high probability of the transference of *spirits; it flows from the top*. If he or she is laying hands on you there is a 100% chance of spiritual transference.

The only way this will not happen is by the Mercy of God and or if your spirit man is stronger than what is coming at you.

The congregants are spellbound and are candidates for being ripped off, not just in physical offerings, but sometimes in that way. They are candidates for sacrifice--, some marriages are sacrificed whether the pastor is breaking up marriages or not—and he or she can and will if they want to. Wherever they got their powers, they owe that power and must do what it now says. So when the priest of an altar gets power from a demonic source, that demon is now running the "church" with the "pastor" as the front man.

It's over, folks. It just hasn't all happened yet. It may take some time, but it is over. The congregants are all at risk to be candidates for sacrifice; the demon wants blood and Christian blood is most appealing to them.

You'd better know where you are "worshipping," and that Jehovah God is the LORD of that church and no other.

Folks, you can't just go anywhere that is called, *church*. You can't just go anywhere with a steeple or a cross affixed to the building. Your Earth life, your eternal destination, and the lives of your children and your *children's* children depend on what church you attend and what leadership you sit under.

Unless you are fully in Christ and solidly bold as a Christian with your own prayer covering, serving God to the utmost and in the whole armor of God, even in a so-called church, who or what the "pastor" is worshipping is also who you are worshipping. By sitting under him (or her), you are initiated into what they are serving.

Are people living or dying in that place? I ask that again because when demons want blood and makes that demand to the one who owes them for favors, that compromised person won't volunteer himself or his family--, usually.... **You had better stay prayed up, anyway.** If people are dying mysteriously in a church, fast and pray. Ask the Lord what you should do and if you should stay or go? People, even those in leadership who have made deals with the devil must service the evil altar that is providing --- whatever their deal was about with blood.

Sounds dramatic but pray and let the Holy Ghost lead you. If you are to get out of there, then get out. Renounce and denounce all association with that place. Break all soul ties with the pastor, the leadership, the building, the congregants, the altar, in the Name of Jesus.

Choose By the Altar

Choose the altar that God *sends* you to. Choose the Altar that allows you to interface with the Spirit of God. Choose the altar that translates your sacrifices unto the Lord, that Jesus can make intercession for us in so doing and worship the Father in proxy. Choose the altar that in turn, like Jacob's ladder allows the spiritual ministers of God to scale up and down to bring the blessings of God to you, without adding sorrow with it. Choose the altar, then all the stuff that goes around the altar will automatically come with the altar – the "church." **Don't choose the church—,**

the exterior trappings, choose the altar--, the interior workings.

Choose the Godly altar that produces Godly results and Godly fruit—all others, shun.

Choose to worship the Lord in Spirit and in Truth; He is looking for those who will do just that. Choose the one true God, the Only Living God; choose a real church with One Altar--, a clean and Godly altar.

If God has *sent* you to sacrifice on an altar, do that.

If God calls you to support an altar, do that.

If God calls you to support an altar, do that.

If God says this is the altar for you and your family, stay there.

If God has *sent* you to cry out against an altar, do that.

If God has *sent* you to see a thing and file a spiritual report and keep your mouth shut, do that.

If God has *sent* you to turn over an altar, desecrate an evil altar, or even destroy it, do that. But only do it if He *sent* you.

If God calls you to **leave** an altar because it is not expedient for you to be there, or be there in this season, do that. Even if everything looks normal and great and pretty, and churchy, but God said, ***Go***, then you go.

If God sends you to tear up an altar, do that. Do not go around town with a sledgehammer, unless God said do that. Most often, we do altar work required by God, in prayers, spiritual warfare, declarations, and decrees.

It doesn't matter if that church is old and elegant, contemporary and modern. If it has nice people in it or rich people in it, or poor people in it – today. If the altar is alive and well all that will change and those people will begin to become sons of God, looking more like Jesus daily, putting on the nature of Christ.

If that altar is not of God, no matter how beautiful the building is or how well the pastor dresses and speaks, eventually it will fall. God will send a prophet to cry out against that altar sooner or later, either audibly or as a watchman in the spirit, and that house of cards will come tumbling down.

Choose the altar that God tells you to choose and be joined to that place to the praise of God's glory. Amen.

On This Revelation

Who do men say that I am?

Thou art the Christ, says Peter.

Jesus said, Flesh and blood hath not revealed that to you, and ***on this revelation I will build my Church and the gates of hell shall not prevail against it.***

On a hill far away, stood an old, rugged Cross, the emblem of suffering and shame. On that Cross hung a man who knew no sin but took on all of ours to reconcile us back to the Father. Men ought to always call on the Lord. But God has said there will come a time when men will call but they will not find Him.

Still, we call on Him. The greatest of all Altars was that old, rugged Cross but it was not an altar until there was a sacrifice on it. That sacrifice was the greatest of all sacrifices ever. And when that sacrifice was consumed, in the natural, it so moved the heart of God that He arose and came to that Altar and to that situation of sin-sick, and lost mankind, and specifically His own Son who needed to be resurrected. God arose, and when God arose, Jesus arose. Jesus had already told us that the Father and I are One. When God arose, Jesus arose.

Saints of God, if you are in Christ, and Christ is in you; when God arises, you arise. You arise out of the depths of loneliness, depression, poverty, sickness—whatever situation you are going through. When your sacrifice is pleasing to God, when your sacrifice, your offering impresses God, He will arise and come to it.

Once He is there, <u>you</u> arise.

You will no longer be beneath, but on top. You will no longer be sick, but in health. You will no longer be the last, but now the first. Your whole situation will change to be like Him when you are in Him and He is in You.

When the One who loves you so much says, **Meet me at the altar and I will meet you there**; He is faithful. He comes to that Godly altar when you are there at the appointed time, with your proper sacrifice, in the Name of Jesus. Your proper acts of faith and worship impress God, and He will arise. He will arise to save you, help you, rescue you, redeem you, heal you. Your sacrifice can move Him, but He is also moved by His great heart of compassion and Love toward you. He will arise to help you. **AMEN.**

Dear Reader

Thank you for acquiring and reading this book. I pray it will be a help to you when you are looking for a church home.

I pray it will be a help when you are looking at the altar that holds the key to your spirituality, your spiritual life, your health, finances, and hearing every Word that proceeds from the mouth of God.

In the Name of Jesus,

Amen.

Dr. Marlene Miles

Prayer books by this author

While most books by this author have prayer points either throughout the book or at the end, there are some books that are **only** prayers. You just open up the book and pray. They are listed below:

Prayers Against Barrenness: *For Success in Business and Life*

Fruit of the Womb: *Prayers Against Barrenness*

Beauty Curses, *Warfare Prayers Against*
https://a.co/d/5Xlc20M

Courts of Marriage: Prayers for Marriage in the Courts of Heaven
(prayerbook) https://a.co/d/cNAdgAq

Courtroom Warfare @ Midnight
(prayerbook) https://a.co/d/5fc7Qdp

Demonic Cobwebs *(prayerbook)*
https://a.co/d/fp9Oa2H

Every Evil Bird https://a.co/d/hF1kh1O

Every Evil Arrow
https://a.co/d/afgRkiA

Gates of Thanksgiving

I Call Down Fire (new!)
https://a.co/d/hN7kGnE

Spirits of Death & the Grave, Pass Over Me and My House
https://a.co/d/dS4ewyr

Please note that my name is spelled incorrectly on amazon, but not on the book.

Throne of Grace: Courtroom Prayer

https://a.co/d/fNMxcM9

Warfare Prayer Against Poverty

https://a.co/d/bZ61IYu

Other books by this author

AK: *The Adventures of the Agape Kid*

AMONG SOME THIEVES

Ancestral Powers https://a.co/d/9prTyFf

Backstabbers https://a.co/d/gi8iBxf

Barrenness, *Prayers Against* https://a.co/d/feUltIs

Battlefield of Marriage, *The*

Blindsided: *Has the Old Man Bewitched You?* https://a.co/d/5O2fLLR

Break Free from Collective Captivity

Casting Down Imaginations
https://a.co/d/1UxlLqa

Churchzilla, The Wanna-Be, Supposed-to-be Bride of Christ

Curses of Blind Men

Demonic Cobwebs (prayerbook)

Demonic Time Bombs

Demons Hate Questions

Devil Loves Trauma, *The*

Devil Weapons: Unforgiveness, Bitterness,...

The Devourers: Thieves of Darkness 2

Do Not Swear by the Moon

Don't Refuse Me, Lord (4 book series)
https://a.co/d/idP34LG

Dream Defilement

The Emptiers: *Thieves of Darkness, 1*
https://a.co/d/5I4n5mc

Every Evil Arrow
https://a.co/d/afgRkiA

Evil Touch https://a.co/d/gSGGpS1

Failed Assignment
https://a.co/d/3CXtjZY

Fantasy Spirit Spouse
https://a.co/d/hW7oYbX

FAT Demons (The): *Breaking Demonic Curses*

The Fold (5-book series)

- The Fold (Book 1)
- Name Your Seed (Book 2)
- The Poor Attitudes of Money (3)
- Do Not Orphan Your Seed (4)
- For the Sake of the Gospel (5)
- My Sowing Journal

Gang Ups: Touch Not God's Anointed

got HEALING? Verses for Life

got LOVE? Verses for Life

got HOPE? Verses for Life

got money? https://a.co/d/g2av41N

How to Dental Assist

How to Dental Assist2: Be Productive, Not Wasteful

I Take It Back

Legacy

Let Me Have A Dollar's Worth
https://a.co/d/h8F8XgE

Level the Playing Field

Living for the NOW of God

Lose My Location
https://a.co/d/crD6mV9

Man Safari, *The*

Marriage Ed. Rules of Engagement & Marriage

Made Perfect in Love

Money Hunters: Beware of Those

Money on the Altar https://a.co/d/4EqJ2Nr

Mulberry Tree https://a.co/d/9nR9rRb

Motherboard (The) - *Soul Prosperity Series*

Name Your Seed

Occupy: *Until I Return*

Plantation Souls

Players Gonna Play

Power Money: Nine Times the Tithe

https://a.co/d/gRt41gy

The Power of Wealth *(forthcoming)*

Powers Above

The Robe, Part 1, The Lessons of Joseph

The Robe, Part II, The Lessons of Joseph

Seasons of Grief

Seasons of Waiting

Seasons of War

Second Marriage, Third--, *Any Marriage*

https://a.co/d/6m6GN4N

Sift You Like Wheat

Six Men Short: What Has Happened to all the Men?

Soul Prosperity soul prosperity series 3

https://a.co/d/5p8YvCN

Souls Captivity soul prosperity series 2

The Spirit of Poverty

StarStruck

SUNBLOCK

The Swallowers: *Thieves of Darkness*, 3

Take It Back

This Is NOT That: How to Keep Demons from Coming at You

Time Is of the Essence

Too Many Wives: *Why You Have Lady Problems*

Tormenting Spirits https://a.co/d/dAogEJf

Toxic Souls

Triangular Power *(series)*

- Powers Above
- SUNBLOCK
- Do Not Swear by the Moon
- STARSTRUCK

Uncontested Doom

Unguarded Hours, *The*

Unseen Life, *The*
https://a.co/d/0drZ5Ll

Upgrade: How to Get Out of Survival Mode

- Toxic Souls (Book 2 of series)
- Legacy (Book 3 of series)

The Wasters: *Thieves of Darkness,* Bk 2
https://a.co/d/bUvI9Jo

What Have You to Declare? What Do You Have With You from Where You've Been?

When I Was A Child, *I Prayed As a Child*

When the Devourer is Rebuked

https://a.co/d/1HVv8oq

The Wilderness Romance *(series)* This series is about conducting a Godly relationship and marriage with someone who is a Wilderness person. It is about how to recognize it and navigate through it. These books are about how not to get caught up in such.

- *The Social Wilderness*
- *The Sexual Wilderness*
- *The Spiritual Wilderness*

Other Series

The Fold (a series on Godly finances)
https://a.co/d/4hz3unj

Soul Prosperity Series https://a.co/d/bz2M42q

Spirit Spouse books

https://a.co/d/9VehDSo

https://a.co/d/97sKOwm

Thieves of Darkness series

Triangular Powers https://a.co/d/aUCjAWC

Upgrade (series) *How to Get Out of Survival Mode* https://a.co/d/aTERhX0